GW01454188

MYKONOS MADE ME DO IT

DIMITRIS MARGETAS

MYKONOS MADE ME DO IT
© 2025 DIMITRIS MARGETAS

All rights reserved.
No part of this publication may be reproduced, stored in a
retrieval system, or transmitted in any form or by any means—
electronic, mechanical, photocopying, or otherwise—without the
prior written permission of the publisher.

This work is a product of fiction, humour, and personal
experience. Any resemblance to actual persons, living or dead, or
to actual events beyond widely reported news, is purely
coincidental.

First Edition: 2025

Dedicated to my dad,
Who's my inspiration
of how life should be
and who was the one
who took me to Mykonos
for the first time.

INTRODUCTION

If you've already read the eBook *Mykonos Made Me Do It*, you know what that one's about: the *Top 10s of party places, restaurants, beaches, Influencer spots*, and more. It included survival tips that save your wallet (and your dignity). Plus anecdotes about the island's famous sights, and photos. Lots of photos of beaches, sunsets, and whitewashed alleys that make Mykonos look like paradise.

That eBook is refreshed every year, so it's always up to date — a guide that helps you plan, book, and brag.

But let's be honest: the eBook is the polished version. Glossy, curated, a safe entry into the island. It gives you the Mykonos that looks good on Instagram — beautiful, organized, helpful.

This paperback is something else entirely. This is the uncut version. It's raw, funny, sometimes absurd, and always honest. Think of this paperback as a backstage pass. The velvet rope opens, and instead of champagne foam and perfect lighting, you'll see the cables, the chaos, and the messy reality that makes Mykonos unforgettable.

Because deep down, you want the truth. Not the PR version of Mykonos, but the uncensored one. The island is magnetic, absurd, exhausting, intoxicating. One minute you're eating the best grilled octopus of your life, the next you're arguing with a sunbed manager about whether €120 includes a towel. One night you're dancing barefoot under the stars, the next morning you're Googling "cheap ferry out of here."

Because Mykonos isn't just "the island of the winds" or "the Ibiza of Greece." Actually Ibiza is the Mykonos of Spain.

Mykonos has always been a paradox: a place where billionaires and backpackers collide, where romance coexists with scams, and where locals both love and resent the circus. It's paradise with a receipt — and usually a very long one.

Inside, you'll find four things:

- The Mykonos people – Who comes here, who you'll bump into, how to spot them

- Stories – Outrageous nights, unexpected encounters, the things you can't make up. These are my personal stories, dropped into each chapter as humorous breathers between the facts. Think of them as shots of ouzo between the courses — quick, strong, and guaranteed to change the mood.

- Scandals – Because behind the glamour, Mykonos thrives on drama.

- FAQ – The questions people ask me and Google every single summer, answered without filters.

Final Warning

Read on if you want to laugh, gasp, and maybe cry a little. But don't say I didn't warn you: after this book, you may never look at Mykonos the same way again. And yet, somehow, you'll still want to go.

Because no matter how many scandals I reveal, no matter how much chaos I describe… in the end, Mykonos always wins.

So pour yourself a drink, and let's dive in.

THE PEOPLE OF MYKONOS

What I mean with "the people of Mykonos" is who comes to Mykonos, who you will find here, who will be at the next umbrella at the beach, who will steal your Nammos table, and who you'll end up sharing a cab with at 4 a.m.

If you know your surroundings you feel safer. You also organize your own game better.

I will be insightful. I will refrain myself from stating the obvious. Yes, there are lots of escorts in Mykonos. You know that. I should not spend space, ink and printing money to profile them. You have them in your cities, you meet them at the hottest spots, you get introduced to them by your bachelor friends. Some of your friends might even freelance in that line of work. Check for the good-looking ones. I have met a few. They are wonderful people. But pls stop asking me if I know any escorts and how much they charge. I am a gyros entrepreneur and a notable author. I am not a pimp.

So I will present to you the 10 archetypes of Mykonos human beings, so once you spot them, you decide either get closer to them or slowly and discreetly distance yourself, for your own reasons.

The Instagram Honeymooners

They came for romance. At least, that's what the wedding registry said when Aunt Maria paid for their flights. But somewhere between check-in at the villa and their third "golden hour" photo shoot, the honeymoon turned into unpaid modeling work.

They've been planning this since October—every restaurant, every beach club, every "secret spot" already bookmarked. Their daily schedule looks like a military operation. In just 2.5 days they must conquer:

- Scorpios for sunset ritual
- Spilia for the white towels waving
- Nammos for the champagne spray
- Interni for dinner "under the lights"
- Alemagou for boho credibility
- Noema for the minimalist Instagram grid
- Delos for fake culture
- Little Venice for the kissing photo
- plus shopping in Chora to prove they "supported local."

They will spend €3,000 in three days—but don't worry, they share the cost. That's what love is all about, after all.

And then? They'll vanish. Off to a cheaper Greek island for a week of recovery. Mykonos was never meant to be their holiday. It was their performance.

They come from everywhere—Germany, Texas, Argentina—but they all have the same look: slightly stressed, slightly broke, slightly sunburned, but still smiling for the camera.

Here's the funny part: they believe that everyone in Mykonos lives like they do. They imagine that locals and week-long visitors spend everyday sprinting between Alemagou and Nammos, booking cabanas, chasing sunsets, and dropping thousands as if it's nothing. To them, anyone who can survive here for more than three days must be a millionaire.

At dinner they don't talk. They order two always different plates, photograph them from five different directions, post, and then quietly eat in silence while refreshing for likes.

Locals watch this ritual with a mix of horror and amusement. "They're not married to each other," one waiter mutters. "They're married to their phones."

How to spot them: matching white outfits, one posing and the other snapping, both dead tired, but glowing on Instagram.

"SURPRISE! AGAIN."

At sunset in Little Venice, a man drops to one knee. Gasps. Phones come out. The crowd claps. She looks shocked.

Tears. Hand to chest. Pure magic. Then she whispers something.

He nods. Gets up. They reset.

Two minutes later:

TAKE 2.

Same gasp. Same knee. This time, she angles herself toward the light. "Better," she says, reviewing footage.

"But let's try one with the wind in my hair."

TAKE 3.

He proposes again while she slowly turns like a rotating mezze platter.

By TAKE 4, the crowd has stopped clapping. The drone's battery dies mid-spin. the waiter is hiding behind a wine barrel cannot deliver the orders, the ice is melting in the glasses.

Final take nailed. She says yes. Again. She finally gets the shot. He's still kneeling—less romantic now, more orthopedic emergency.

They leave without ordering. Was it real? Was it content?

Nobody knows. But that ring's seen more action than my underwear.

Love is beautiful. But lighting? Crucial.

MYKONOS MADE THEM DO IT

"PERSONAL PHOTOGRAPHER"

They asked me to take a beach photo—simple, right?

I took three confident steps back, lined up the perfect shot…

And tripped on my own flip-flop.

The phone flew from my hand like it had wings—

Straight into the sea. Splash. Gone.

I panicked.

They stared at the water, then looked at me and shrugged:

"Honestly? It was an old phone. I hated it. You did me a favor."

Relieved but guilty, I offered to pay.

They said, "No need. But you owe me something else…"

And that's how I became their personal photographer for the entire weekend.

Sunsets, cocktails, beach jumps, outfit changes—I was a one-man paparazzi.

I tried to escape once.

They said, "Not until I have a new profile pic that slaps."

I paid my debt in 1,374 photos.

MYKONOS MADE ME DO IT

The Billionaires & Celebrities

They don't stay in Mykonos. They occupy it.

They arrive by yacht, by helicopter, or sometimes both—just to make a point. Their accommodation is a villa with twenty bedrooms, either rented at astronomical rates or borrowed from someone even richer. Some villas are so huge they're practically villages, complete with security, chefs, and a fleet of black SUVs lined up outside.

Wherever they go, they don't just book a table. They book half the place. At Scorpios, they'll quietly reserve an entire section. At Nammos, they'll casually block ten cabanas so their friends can "drop by."

They are either famous Americans, Russian oligarchs, or Emirates royalty. Some are officially "on holiday." Others are unofficially doing business deals between magnum bottles of rosé. All of them know that Mykonos isn't just about nightlife—it's about visibility.

They pretend to be incognito, hiding behind oversized sunglasses. But the truth is, the photographers were tipped off hours before they landed. Their PR isn't in the photos, though—it's in the tips. A €10,000 gratuity at a restaurant becomes legend overnight.

And then there's the medical staff. Twice a day, private doctors make villa visits to inject them with vitamins, antioxidants, and other "legal enhancers" to keep them looking fresh. It's the only way they can continue consuming illegal enhancers—plus alcohol in volumes that would kill a mortal.

The girlfriends? Let's just say they're "recently renovated." Perfect cheekbones, identical handbags, and a sense of timing that suggests they know exactly when the cameras are rolling.

Whether you call them billionaires or celebrities doesn't matter—they behave the same. The goal isn't to relax in Mykonos. The goal is to remind the world they were here.

How to spot them: Arrival of convoy of black SUVs, security guys with earpieces looking "casual" in designer polos, drones hovering (paparazzi or their own film crew).

"MMM"

I arrived in Mykonos, tired, but excited. At the hotel reception, the guy squints at his screen and says,

"Ah! You must be with Mr. Matinakis's group?"

Now—I could correct him. But instead, I just smile politely and say, "Mmm." That's it. Just a mysterious Mmm. They hand me a welcome drink, call me "sir" way too many times, and escort me to a massive suite with a sea view, robes softer than clouds, and even a pillow menu.

I live my best accidental billionaire life for two full days.

Then Friday morning hits. The phone rings.

"Your helicopter will be ready at noon to take you to your gathering."

Panic. Silence. Guilt.

I head to reception, sunglasses on, shame off. I whisper,

"So… slight mix-up… I'm not actually with Mr. Matinakis group."

They smile too professionally, and fifteen minutes later, I'm carrying my bag to a perfectly fine—but very normal—room with no sea view and one flat pillow.

Still, I regret nothing.

MYKONOS MADE ME DO IT

"OPA OVERLOAD"

At first, it was cute. Every clink of glasses:

"Opa!"

Big smile. Big energy. Tourist charm.

By the tenth time, the table next to him stopped cheers-ing.

By the twentieth, a waiter flinched.

By the thirty-second "Opa!", the manager walked over and whispered,

"Sir... please. No more joy."

He paused, nodded respectfully—

Then raised his glass one last time and whispered:

"Opa." Like it was a funeral.

For fun.

MYKONOS MADE HIM DO IT

The Rich Divorcée

They arrive in Mykonos freshly untethered, eager to rewrite the script of their lives. Divorce, for them, is not the end—it's a second adolescence. One with better credit cards.

For the men, the party life is brand new. They never drank much before, but now that nobody's watching, they drink like sailors. At first, they believe their charm and "great personality" will land them a stunning twenty-five-year-old. It takes them four days to realize that in Mykonos, personality isn't currency. Only money is. By day five, they're looking for paid company, the transaction smoothing over the bruises of rejection.

The women reinvent themselves as social butterflies with plumped lips and collagen-filled confidence. They overdress for every occasion, glittering with jewellery that competes with the sunset. But other women aren't allies here. Other women are competition. They're all fishing in the same champagne-soaked pool.

So the Rich Divorcée women look elsewhere for companionship. Gay men become the perfect accessory: fun, stylish, endlessly flattering, and great for photo ops. Beside them, she shines, unchallenged and admired, without the risk of rivalry.

Whether male or female, divorcées in Mykonos are united by one trait: they cannot stand being alone. When the party ends, when the staff leave the table, when the rented companion slips away, they collapse into silence they cannot bear.

They tell endless stories—about status, money, villas, yachts, exes, and glamorous tragedies. The men brag about past conquests. The women brag about who they once dined with in Saint-Tropez.

They stay for a week, usually in a chic hotel where they immediately flirt with the staff. And they always come back, convinced that they "belong here" — that the island, with its glitter and excess, is their natural habitat.

How to spot them: overdressed at breakfast, lips inflated beyond biology, telling stories louder than the music, and never, ever sitting alone.

"TWO CLUBS, ONE DRAMA QUEEN"

We hit the first bar — flashy, posh, and packed. that place where the music's so loud you can feel it in your bones, and the drinks are served with a side of "please don't spill it on my Balenciaga."

We're four in total: two guys, two girls, all in our 40s, and all in the mood to have a blast.

Well, almost all of us.

The vibe? Electric. The crowd? Wild.

But one of our group? Not having it.

"Nothing is happening," she says, arms crossed, like she's in the middle of a book club meeting.

The place is on fire, but she's only looking for one thing: attention. If no one's looking at her, it's a bad night. Classic.

"Nothing is happening," she says, and I look around. Well, honey, the place is buzzing, but you're not getting the attention you crave. I thought that, I did not tell her.

You know those friends who think a good night only counts if someone's hitting on them? Yeah, that's her.

If nobody's making eye contact or sending a drink her way, it's like the night doesn't even exist.

We bail and head to a Greek music club. We're vibing, dancing, laughing, living our best lives.

She?

Frowning, scanning the crowd like she's at a thrift store.

"This place is too young and poor," she mutters.

Yeah, we heard that.

She tries to convince her friend to leave. No luck.

She tries me? Nope, I'm dancing like it's my last night on Earth.

She even goes to the other guy, the most accommodating of us. He pretends he can't hear her over the music — classic move.

Finally, she storms off alone.

The rest of us? We end up at Cavo Paradiso, catching Peggy Gou as the sun comes up.

Best night ever.

Sunrise comes, and let me tell you, it was like watching a movie — we're all alive, soaking in the last hours of the night, while she's probably sulking at home, Googling "Best place to find rich men in Mykonos."

MYKONOS MADE HER DO IT

"AT THE TABLE NEXT TO US"

Girl: "Does taramasalata have dairy?"

Waiter: "No."

Girl: "Are you positive? Like, zero dairy traces? No feta floating through the air?"

Waiter: "It's fish roe, lemon, olive oil. No dairy."

Girl: "Because last time I had tzatziki, I blacked out at a wedding."

Friend: "No, babe. You blacked out because you took six shots of ouzo and tried to flirt with the priest."

Girl: "It started with the dairy. I felt a tingle."

Friend: "That was the priest blessing you from a distance."

Girl: "Okay. I'll skip the tarama." (pause) "I'll just have the spinach pie. But can you remove the feta crumbles inside? Just to be safe."

Waiter: (blinks) "You want… us to remove the feta… from inside the spinach pie?"

Girl: "Yes. Just scoop it out or something."

Waiter: (losing grip on reality) "It's… melted… into the spinach…"

Girl: "Okay, then just do your best."

Waiter: (silently walks away) —returns thirty seconds later with a second waiter— "This is my colleague. He'll be taking over."

MYKONOS MADE HER DO IT

The Influencer in the Wild

For the Influencer, Mykonos isn't a destination — it's a backdrop. The island is not experienced, it is curated. Every moment, every plate of food, every breeze is an opportunity to generate content.

They arrive with more equipment than luggage: ring lights, drones, tripods. Their suitcase isn't full of clothes; it's full of outfits. Ten changes a day, carefully organized for specific locations.

If they are a little famous, they'll stay in a random "room to let" two hours outside Ano Mera — free, of course — in exchange for a glowing post. If they are really famous, then Soula will swoop in and place them at Cavo Tagoo.

They're always on the hunt for freebies: free meals, free sunbeds, free clothes. But above all, they want proximity to real celebrities. Because a selfie with a billionaire, DJ, or actor will get them views.

The truth is, nobody in Mykonos actually knows them. Maybe a handful of followers from their own country might recognize them — and even that is rare, since most of their fans couldn't afford a coffee on the island.

They don't party much. Nights are for post-production. While everyone else is dancing barefoot at 6 a.m., they're hunched over a laptop, editing and scheduling so the next morning's post is ready.

They're never alone. They're always attached to a local — someone who introduces them around as, "This is Mary, she's a famous TikToker in Mozambique." The local gets some glam, but pays for their drinks and taxis.

During their stay, they flood their stories with praise: "so glam, so cool, so beautiful." But the moment they leave, they post a jaded critique: "Honestly? Mykonos is overrated. Nothing special."

How to spot them: holding up an entire street in Chora, changing outfits in public bathrooms, tagging every brand in sight.

"THIS IS MY SECRET SPOT"

She walked into the beach bar like she owned the island.

Big hat, tiny bikini, full glam. She stopped right in the middle of the crowd, raised her phone, and loudly declared:

"This is my secret spot. I never tell anyone about this place!"

She shouted this over a DJ set.

At a bar with a two-hour waiting list.

Where every sunbed had a reserved sign and three influencers already tagging it in Stories.

People looked up from their cocktails like, whose secret is this, exactly?

She repeated it five times while filming herself walking in slow motion—past packed tables, a wedding party, and three people filming her filming herself.

Then she left. Didn't order. Didn't sit. Just said:

"Ugh, too crowded now. Not the vibe." Yes, babe. Probably because you told everyone.

MYKONOS MADE HER DO IT

"THE TWO-HOUR TIME TRAP"

At the next table, the debates started immediately: Wine or cocktails?

"I want a mojito!"

"No, rosé all the way!"

"Why not both?"

Then, once the wine camp won, came which wine:

"Pinot Grigio!"

"Sauvignon Blanc!"

"Wait, chilled or room temp?"

Next, the big question: Food to share or each their own? The debate quickly turned into all fish or all meat?

"The fish here is incredible!"

"But the lamb is legendary!"

After nearly two hours of debate, the food finally arrived — and the photoshoot began.

Angles, boomerangs, stories, filters — the food barely got a bite.

Before they could eat, the waiter slid the bill across: "Time to go!"

They boxed up their food to take away and rushed off, carrying their meals like trophies — straight to the clubs. But none of the clubs let them in. Denied at every door.

I later spotted them at Paraportiani, sitting on the steps — a spot known for late-night escapades — eating their food under the stars.

The perfect Mykonos ending: hungry, rejected, and dining with a side of romance in the moonlight.

Mykonos lesson: Two-hour dinners are a race, and clubs don't do leftovers — but Paraportiani welcomes all kinds of nights.

MYKONOS MADE ME DO IT

The Party Veteran

This is not their first summer in Mykonos. It's not even their tenth. For the Party Veteran, Mykonos is less of a destination and more of a long-term relationship — complicated, expensive, but impossible to quit.

There are two main tribes:

1. The Scandinavian Fanatics

Despite the name, they're not all Scandinavian. Many are Italians who just party like Scandinavians. They travel in packs — either groups of only girls or only boys — and arrive with a single purpose: to squeeze every beat out of the island. They dance until sunrise, collapse into sleep, wake up late, eat almost nothing, and repeat.

2. The Scorpios/Alemagou Loyalists

This group skews older, often couples who've decided that life is best lived to the rhythm of tribal drums. Sunset rituals at Scorpios, sand-between-your-toes nights at Alemagou, cocktails that somehow taste like spirituality mixed with tequila.

Both tribes have one sacred pilgrimage in common: Cavo Paradiso at sunrise. The Veteran doesn't see it as a club — it's a temple. Watching the sun rise over the sea while still dancing is not just a tradition. It's a baptism, repeated every summer.

And always, the sunglasses. They hide hangovers, shield against sunrise regret, and let them keep nodding along even when their eyes gave up hours ago.

Their bodies run on minimal food, maximum alcohol, and an unholy amount of day-sleep. Their "dinners" happen at dawn. Either a full hotel breakfast before finally collapsing into bed, or a hearty souvlaki at Jimmy's. Nobody remembers the entire night, but the story is reconstructed piece by piece the next afternoon, over coffee at 2:30 p.m.

How to spot them: sunglasses at night, barefoot at sunrise, still smiling while everyone else is limping home.

"FOUR-STAR HOTEL, FIVE-STAR TRAUMA"

I got back from Thalami at 9 a.m. I was done. Dead. Desperate for sleep. I hang the sign on the door: DO NOT DISTURB

In bed. Heaven.

Ten minutes later: Knock knock. "Housekeeping!".

"No, thank you!" I yell from the pillow.

An hour later. Knock knock. "Housekeeping!"

Still polite, but louder: "NO THANK YOU!"

Round three? No knock. Just the click of the door unlocking and a woman walking in with towels like she owned the place.

Round four? Same. She walked in, saw me in bed, and asked cheerfully, "Fresh towels?"

I waved one hand: "Please... no."

By the fifth knock, I sprang out of bed in full drama mode— underwear, one sock, hair looking like I'd fought a leaf blower, and opened the door mid-rage:

"CAN YOU NOT READ?!"

The maid blinked, then showed me the sign hang outside: PLEASE CLEAN MY ROOM I stared at it. I stared at her. She smiled. "Okay now?"

It wasn't. I reversed the sign, crawled back to bed, and immediately got a message: "We're outside! Beach time!"

So I threw on my swimsuit, flipped the sign to PLEASE CLEAN MY ROOM, and left.

Came back hours later.

Room? Still a disaster.

Bed? Still a crumpled crime scene.

Towels? Still emotionally damp.

They never cleaned it. Not that day. Not the next.

I left the sign up the whole time, just in case. They left it right there with me—like a souvenir of my sleep-deprived humiliation.

MYKONOS MADE ME DO IT

"THE BLUETOOTH BANDIT"

So I spotted this guy on the beach with a big Bluetooth speaker.

He was playing it loud. Too loud. But not good music—just endless deep house loops with zero personality.

And guess what? He wasn't taking requests.

So I did what any mature adult in Mykonos would do:

I hijacked it. I connected my phone...

And played Samantha Fox – "Touch Me"—the moaning version.

It blasted across the beach.

Everyone turned.

Kids. Grandmas. One nun (I swear).

People gasped.

And the poor guy? He froze. Mortified.

He scrambled to pause it, looked at his phone—nothing.

I marched over, acting outraged:

"Excuse me! There are children here!"

He apologized. To me. I told him to show some respect.

Then walked away...

...and played "I Wanna Sex You Up."

MYKONOS MADE ME DO IT

The Budget Conscious Explorer

They made it to Mykonos against all odds. Flights were expensive, hotels were outrageous, cocktails cost the price of a scooter rental — but they were determined. You can't tell people you've "done Greece" without posting at least one picture from Mykonos.

From the moment they land, the calculator never leaves their hand. Every choice is weighed in euros: "If we take a taxi, that's two gyros gone." Their favorite sentence is: "Can we just share one?"

They stay in modest pensions or Airbnbs far from the action, usually somewhere the bus stops only twice a day. When they do take the bus, they glare at the €2.30 ticket like it's highway robbery. Sunbeds at €40? Forget it. They'll spread a towel in the worst corner of the beach, pretending they "prefer the authentic side."

Meals are an exercise in restraint. Gyros and supermarket snacks sustain them, with maybe one "real dinner" squeezed into the trip. A single cocktail is a once-in-a-holiday indulgence, stretched out for hours with sips so tiny you'd think they were tasting poison.

They're convinced there must be a "secret cheap Mykonos" that locals hide from tourists — some hidden taverna where souvlaki is €3, drinks are €5, and sunbeds are free. They ask every waiter, taxi driver, and kiosk owner about it. The answer never changes: "It doesn't exist."

Yet back home, none of this matters. Their Instagram still says "Mykonos ⚚✦" with a beach photo carefully framed to hide the fact that their towel was squeezed between two trash cans. Nobody knows they survived on bread, beer, and resentment. To their followers, they were in paradise.

How to spot them: sitting on a towel instead of a sunbed, rationing supermarket wine like it's Dom Pérignon, and calculating bills with deadly focus.

"SHARED BALCONY, SHARED TRAUMA"

Day One in Mykonos. I'm blissfully asleep, dreaming of tiropita and beach shots — until I'm jolted awake by:

"AND SQUEEZE THOSE GLUTES, LADIES!"

I stumble to the balcony. There she is: leggings, laptop, and too much enthusiasm.

My neighbor has turned our shared balcony into a sunrise Pilates studio. Day Two, it happens again—8:00 a.m. sharp.

She's mid-burpee, I'm mid-panic.

I ask politely, "Hey, any chance we can shift the glute-squeezing to, say... the afternoon?"

She smiles and says, "Non! The instructor is in Bali. This is the afternoon for her." Fantastic.

Day Three. I wake up before the shouting. I make coffee. I stretch.

She arrives, surprised. "You're joining?"

I nod, roll out my towel, and mutter,

"I figured if you can't beat 'em…"

Somewhere between lunges and hangover, I blacked out emotionally. First. Then physically. Thankfully that was her last day on the island...

MYKONOS MADE ME DO IT

"FLUSH AND UPLOAD"

My friend stayed at a hostel in Mykonos where the Wi-Fi was… moody. Except for one sacred place: the bathroom.

Not just near it. Inside it. The signal there was so strong you could stream Netflix, call your mom, AND upload a full Instagram carousel—all at once. So naturally, the bathroom became the social hub.

People weren't going in to go. They went in with laptops, snacks, even yoga mats.

One guy gave a full Zoom interview from the toilet seat. Another girl brought a ring light.

At one point, my friend had to knock and ask,

"Sorry—are you actually using the bathroom or editing a reel?"

She replied, "I'm sending invoices." There was a schedule. A sign-up sheet.

Whispers in the hallway:

"Is the Wi-Fi throne free?"

"No, Luca's in there. He's live on Omegle."

It wasn't a hostel anymore. It was a co-working space with occasional flushing. People were knocking on the door like it was a conference room.

By check-out, people left great reviews… for the toilet.

MYKONOS MADE THEM DO IT

The Yacht People

The Yacht People don't just arrive in Mykonos — they stage an entrance. Boats line up side by side in the marina like a floating showroom. If your yacht is smaller than the one next to you, you move. Nothing kills the vibe faster than being dwarfed by a floating palace.

They don't say, "We came by yacht." They don't have to. Within hours, you'll be invited aboard. That's the proof. The invitation isn't about hospitality — it's branding. Step onto the deck, snap a photo, and you've confirmed their status for them.

Their favorite beaches aren't the quiet ones like Agios Sostis. They choose Psarou, Ornos, Paraga — places where the entire island can watch them come and go by tender. Arrivals and departures are runway moments, carefully choreographed so everyone on shore wonders, "Who's on that boat?"

Everyone tries to figure it out. The names of the yachts are googled obsessively, just in case it's a billionaire, a royal, or a celebrity. The mystery is half the entertainment. And those giant satellites stacked on top? They're as impressive as the yacht itself — glowing beacons of wealth and Wi-Fi.

Life on board looks like paradise, but the reality is different. Space is tighter than it appears, and being trapped together 24/7 breeds irritation. The rich aren't easy people. Tempers flare, assistants are scolded, girlfriends sulk. Even luxury starts to feel claustrophobic when you can't escape it.

Still, the show goes on. Yachts here are floating theaters, staged for maximum visibility. Mykonos isn't their destination, it's their audience.

How to spot them: easy — they walk the narrow docks built just for them, or step out of tenders walking like Naomi.

"MAYDAY, MELON DOWN!"

My friend invited us for brunch on the yacht.

Barefoot, shirt open, glistening in enough oil to deep-fry calamari. He arranged the table like a Pinterest dream—fruit, flowers, champagne, full zen mode.

Then he struck a pose and whispered,

"This is life!" Right on cue, a speedboat flew by. The deck jolted.

Croissants took flight.

And my friend—slippery from sunscreen and ego—slid full speed across the deck like a human air hockey puck... ...and landed in a beanbag with a scream and a splash of orange juice. Midair, someone screamed:

"SAVE THE MIMOSA!" The mimosa did not survive.

Neither did the melon.

But the video? Viral. He posted it with the caption:

#YachtLifeIsHard

MYKONOS MADE HIM DO IT

"I HAD NONE"

Partied all night.

Last thing I remember: dancing on a beach table with a guy in a captain's hat.

Next morning, I wake up on a yacht.

In the middle of the sea. Alone. Wearing someone else's sunglasses.

I panicked... until the crew came out and offered me breakfast like this happens every day.

Captain shows up and says,

"You said you needed to escape your ex."

I had no ex.

MYKONOS MADE ME DO IT

The Seasonistas

They don't visit Mykonos — they inhabit it. The Seasonistas are the semi-locals who arrive in May with a backpack, a vague job promise, and way too much optimism.

They're the most professional people on the island — always smiling, polite, and efficient, even when they're running on three hours of sleep.

They arrive in May fresh and enthusiastic — and by October they look ten years older. As of September 1st, they start counting days like prisoners.

Easy to understand the newbies: on day one, they strut to the beach barefoot and shirtless. By day three, the sunburn is so bad they look like lobsters in denim shorts. At the start of the season, they party every night, convinced they'll make a fortune in tips. By mid-August, they're pale from exhaustion, broke, and living off staff meals.

One unwritten rule: they never wear their work clothes outside the job. Either they're not allowed, or they just want to pretend they're normal people again.

Even within the tribe there's a hierarchy: the luxury boutique staff are the glamorous ones, parading around Chora like they're part of the clientele. Meanwhile, the Nammos and Scorpios staff are so drained from twelve-hour shifts of champagne spraying that the last thing you'll ever see them do is go out after work.

They know people. They exchange favors like currency: "Let me into your pool, I'll get you into my beach bar." Beaches are goldmines (drunk groups tip generously), hotels not so much (nobody carries cash in their swimsuit at the pool, especially after paying €1,000 a night for a room).

There are two tribes: the Loyals who return to the same venue every summer, and the Drifters who can change jobs three times in one season. Their accommodation decides everything: a 2 people studio in Ornos means one job, a six-person share-room in Ano Mera means another.

When they're not working, they slip into Agios Yannis, Agios Sostis, or Kapari — or they swim at hotel pools where friendly staff wave them in. In the winter, they migrate like birds, couch-surfing across Europe, hopping between friends they made during the summer.

How to spot them: You don't need to — they'll tell you. Seasonistas are proud of what they do, and they should be: Mykonos is hard work.

"THE FOUREIRA INCIDENT"

Gave my car keys to the valet at a beach club. Cool guy, tight polo, full confidence. Said, "I got you, boss."

Fast forward a few hours and several cocktails, I return to the valet stand. He's there, leaning on the railing like he owns the place.

"Hey," I say. "Can I get my car back?"

"Of course!" he replies. "Give me just a minute."

I give him many minutes. Like... twenty.

No car. No valet. No explanation.

Then I hear screaming—the good kind. The DJ has just dropped a live remix of Eleni Foureira, and the crowd is going wild.

I look over, and there he is: my valet, shirt off, spinning on top of a speaker like he's auditioning for Eurovision.

He's not hiding. He's performing. Turns out, the staff knows all about it. "He does that every time."

Apparently, I just had the bad luck of asking for my car during his big number.

When he finally comes back—sweaty, glowing, and borderline euphoric—he hands me my keys and says,

"Sorry boss, it was the extended live version."

Honestly? I tipped him double. He earned it.

MYKONOS MADE ME DO IT

"OOPS I DID IT AGAIN "

I met someone at a Little Venice bar, things got flirty fast. We kissed.

Moments later, the waiter bringing our drinks sees us, freezes, and says:

"Bro... seriously?"

Yes, seriously I drink it with Coke zero. I thought he was talking about my order...

Turns out they broke up the day before. That was her ex. As of today ex.

She just whispered, "It's Mykonos, babe."

I tipped him 50%. Still not enough.

MYKONOS MADE ME DO IT

The locals don't "do Mykonos." They survive it. For them, summer is not a holiday — it's a season. The circus comes in July and leaves in August, before and after it is fine. They work harder than anyone partying here can imagine.

They complain a lot — about how the island has too many hotels and too many rooms. All this while quietly finishing construction on their fifth bed-and-breakfast. Their parents built Mykonos into what it is today, and they carry that legacy forward with relentless energy.

They are hardworking and sharp — amazing business people who can calculate a season's profit in their head faster than an accountant. Yet they're also discreet. They won't comment on scandals in the press, they don't boast, and they rarely reveal how much they actually own. Many are millionaires, but they don't show it.

They have their own way of enjoying the island. They swim at beaches tourists never find, and when they take holidays themselves, they choose Amorgos — quiet, rugged, unspoiled — the opposite of Mykonos in August. Abroad, they go big: Maldives, Dubai, Tokyo. They also seem to have friends everywhere: Paris, London, New York, São Paulo.

In Mykonos, everyone here is a cousin, niece, or in-law. Family ties run deep, and so does the gossip.

Locals know their loyal clients by name. The families who return every year, the regulars who always book the same villa or table — these clients are treated like true friends. Business and friendship are inseparable here.

And while tourists chase sunsets at Scorpios, locals gather at panigiria, village feasts where music, dancing, and wine last until dawn. In winter, when the island sleeps, you'll find them at the two or three cafés open in Yalos, drinking coffee and planning the next season.

How to spot them: at church; driving a truck through an alley like it's a highway; or quietly running half the island.

"CELEBRITY CONFUSION"

At dinner, people kept waving at her as they walked by — beach club staff, DJs, waiters from three different restaurants.

A tourist at the next table leaned in and asked,

"Are you, like... famous here?"

She smiled and said,

"No, I'm just the voice of Google Maps in Greek. All these people are lost."

He nodded like it made perfect sense.

She didn't correct him.

He asked for a selfie.

She posed and said, "Σε 400 μέτρα, στρίψτε αριστερά."

He gasped.

She didn't break character.

She gave directions to Paradise Beach in her most robotic voice.

MYKONOS MADE HER DO IT

"4-in-1 SNORING STORIES"

Sunbed ASMR

A woman recorded 30 minutes of a man snoring with the waves crashing behind him, labeled it "Beach ASMR" on TikTok, and now has 120k followers. He still has no idea he's famous.

Snore War

Two people fell asleep side by side and started competing snores—one low and grumbly, the other wheezy and high-pitched. People placed bets. I sold popcorn.

The Snore-cerer

A guy snored so loudly on the sunbed, the woman next to him thought he was being possessed. She sprayed Evian on his face and whispered, "The power of Christ compels you." He didn't even flinch—just snored louder.

The Beach Bed Nap

Rented a sunbed at 11 AM. Ordered one spritz. Woke up at 6 PM, mildly sunburned, €240 poorer, with sand in places I can't mention. Apparently, I snored through three DJ sets and a bachelorette photoshoot.

MYKONOS MADE ME DO IT

The Villa Owners

In Athens, they all say, "I have a house in Mykonos." What they really mean is: "I have a business in Mykonos." Villas here aren't homes, they're machines, and the owners know it.

They hardly ever stay in them — unless, of course, the villa goes unrented. When that happens, they suddenly remember the sea air is good for their health. Otherwise, they'll ask to crash at your humble apartment, or hide away in a basic "room to let," all while charging clients €2,000 a night.

They love to talk about their staff — the gardeners, the cleaners, the caretakers. "Impossible to find good people," they sigh, even as the same staff quietly keeps everything running while the owner is back in Kolonaki, counting profits.

On paper, they can provide anything: chefs, drivers, masseuses, yoga instructors, babysitters, DJs. If a client requests it, the villa owner will deliver — at a price. Flexibility is part of the charm. Or at least that's what they tell you.

They pretend to be locals, but they aren't. Most of them used to be tourists who fell in love with Mykonos, then realized the real romance wasn't sunsets — it was rental income. They bought, they built, they expanded. And now? They dominate.

The funniest part: they can't keep secrets. Over cocktails in Athens or London, they tell endless stories about their "guests" — who trashed the pool, who brought five "girlfriends", who left without tipping the staff. Guest confidentiality is an afterthought when gossip is this juicy.

How to spot them: bragging about their "house" in Mykonos, showing up only at check-in and check-out, or casually leaking their guests' private scandals over drinks.

"SLEEP? NOT ON GREG'S WATCH"

I stayed in a beautiful villa in Mykonos. Olive trees, ocean breeze… and one demonic rooster who thought 4:52 a.m. was concert time.

Every. Single. Morning.

"COCK-A-DOODLE—"

My soul left my body.

I complained to the villa owner. They nodded sympathetically… and handed me earplugs like I was the unreasonable one.

Desperate, I went full detective. I stalked the grounds trying to locate him. Nothing. That rooster was a phantom. A feathery ninja.

I even Googled "natural rooster sedatives." I considered blending a Valium smoothie. I never found him, but I imagined him somewhere in the shadows—wide awake, mocking me. So, I flipped the script. If the rooster wanted to start the day at 5 a.m., I would end mine at 6am. Every night, I came home at dawn—open shirt, salty hair, party wristband still on—and greeted that rooster like a coworker.

"Good morning, Greg. Sorry I missed your gig."

We never made peace. But we learned to coexist.

MYKONOS MADE ME DO IT

"SHOULD I?"

I am standing at the stairs of Interni, looking at the crowd having fun. This panoramic view is already viral. I am drinking a whiskey and smoking.

"Should I smack him or her?" I hear next to me.

"Sorry?" was my response when I realized that I was the only one standing next to the pretty girl in beize.

"Do you have a smoke for me?" she asks me while she is still staring at a very specific point in the crowd.

"So him or her?", she goes again, once I lit her ciggie.

She is smart, she understands that the data she provided was too little to offer a substantiated opinion.

"He is my boyfriend and she is a friend. Not my best friend, but one of my friends, we hang out together in London. We came two couples and 2 single gals. She is one of the two."

This is the data she volunteered. Still not enough for me.

"And?"

"And she's been hitting on my boyfriend since we arrived at Mykonos. Now I said I am going to the bathroom. For the last 10 minutes, it looks like the deal is being sealed. So should I slap the asshole or remove the extensions of the slut? This is my question". A

nd now she was staring at me. She wanted an answer.

Normally I would not interfere in the relation of any couple, but this time I did volunteer my wisdom:

"Take him to Nammos Village, max out his credit card and damp him on your way back to London".

MYKONOS MADE ME DO IT

THE SCANDALS

These aren't whispers from a beach bar bathroom — these were in the news. You might have heard them, you might not. But here, you'll get them with **my spin**. The reason I'm putting them all together isn't just for shock value, but to show you how wild Mykonos really is — and how true the island stays to its own brand of chaos.

Because let's be honest:

- Scandals are part of the island's DNA. Without them, Mykonos would just be another beach with overpriced sunbeds.

- They reveal the real Mykonos. Brochures show windmills and sunsets — scandals show what actually happens when too much money, alcohol, and ego share 85 square kilometers.

- They're entertaining. You didn't pick up this book only for restaurant names. A little drama makes the cocktails taste better.

- They're warnings in disguise. If a billionaire can get thrown out of a club, so can you.

- And they prove Mykonos is never boring. Love it, hate it, or both — the island never lets you look away.

Mykonos is a Netflix character: you can't decide if you love it or hate it, but you can't stop watching. Every season brings new drama, fresh scandals, and a plot twist no screenwriter could have invented.

Scandal #1: Holiday Meal Turns Hostage Situation

Every summer, headlines appear like clockwork: "Tourists Shocked by €1,300 Bill in Mykonos." And the story is always the same. A couple sits down at a beachside taverna, no menus in sight, a waiter promises fresh seafood and "free sunbeds," and then—bam—the bill arrives looking like the down payment on a small car.

We're talking €350 for a single fish, €35 for a soft drink, and a casual €1,000+ for the privilege of chewing squid under the Greek sun. And just when the customer thinks it can't get worse, the bill arrives with an outrageous "service charge" or tip automatically added, often hundreds of euros.

Complain? That's when the smiles fade. Guests whisper about being surrounded by broad-shouldered "staff" who make it clear that leaving without paying is not an option.

The irony? Mykonos has never been known as a cheap island. But paying more for calamari than for a flight to Athens—plus tipping enough to pay the waiter's annual electricity bill—is the kind of story that only this island can produce.

Survivors frame their receipt like a war medal. Some even brag about it—because what's more Mykonos than blowing a month's rent on lunch and living to tell the tale?

The moral? On this island, always check the menu, always ask the price, and remember: when someone offers you a "free" sunbed, what they really mean is you're about to fund their new yacht.

"THEY SHOULD SHUT THAT PLACE DOWN"

At a bar, I meet a friend of a friend who works in Mykonos.

We get into a rant about overpriced restaurants.

"There's this one place," I say, "total scam. They rob tourists blind. €140 for a Caesar salad. They smile while they do it. Should be shut down."

He nods. "Ugh, I hate places like that."

"They're thieves. Worst people in Greece", I continue.

"Exactly," he says. "Tourist traps should be banned."

"And the staff… they must be in on it. I mean, to work there, you'd have to be dead inside or just as greedy" is my POV.

"Totally," he says.

"But I can't remember the name… It's the one with the giant lobsters out front… on the beach... near Platis Gialos?"

He pauses. "Wait, do you mean Maré Blu?"

I snap. "YES! That's the one!"

He smiles. "I've worked there for three summers. I really like it. The bosses treat us well. It's a good team."

Silence.

I nod like I've just remembered I left my personality in the taxi.

I tried to swallow my drink and my dignity at the same time. Only one went down.

MYKONOS MADE ME DO IT

"SEAFOOD SHOWDOWN"

She asked if the fish was fresh.

The waiter pointed at the sea and said,

"Of course. He was just swimming 5 minutes ago."

She nodded, impressed.

Until he leaned in and added,

"Not fast enough."

Then offered to show her the fish in the tank.

She followed him — and locked eyes with a grouper that looked like it had seen things.

"I'll have the pasta," she said.

No judgment. No eye contact. No slow swimmers.

MYKONOS MADE HER DO IT

Scandal #2: Cops & Cocaine on the Shoreline

If you thought the biggest crime in Mykonos was a €35 Coca-Cola, think again. In the summer of 2025, the headlines got darker: four police officers—yes, actual police—were arrested for running part of a drug trafficking ring.

According to reports, the officers weren't just looking the other way; they were allegedly stealing confiscated cocaine from evidence lockers and funnelling it back into the island's nightlife. Picture that: the very people meant to keep Mykonos safe were literally supplying the parties they were supposed to police.

It was one of the largest cocaine seizures in Mykonos history, and the scandal shook both the island and Athens. The accused included a sergeant and an inspector—men with years of service, now spending their nights behind bars.

For locals, it wasn't exactly a shock. Mykonos has always been the place where law, money, and temptation meet in messy ways. But to see uniformed officers hauled off in handcuffs? That was next-level irony. The people meant to protect the tourists were apparently helping them dance a little longer.

Of course, the tabloids had a field day. Some called it "The Mykonos Narcos." Others joked that the cops simply wanted to be closer to the music. Whatever the spin, the story confirmed a suspicion many already had: in Mykonos, the line between order and chaos is as thin as a rolled-up banknote.

The moral? Mykonos is full of characters — just don't assume you know who's playing which part.

"THE SEARCH"

So, my best friend and I — in our 40s but looking totally like in our 30s — roll up to Skandinavian.

The crowd? Much younger. But hey, we know the bouncers, so we glide past the line like VIPs.

We're about to step inside when the girl at the door stops us with a serious question:

"Are you looking for your kid?"

We freeze, give her our best austere look, and walk right past.

Fast forward four hours of pure clubbing bliss. We're leaving, still buzzing, when there she is again — the door girl.

We approach her, our faces dead serious.

"We've been looking for our kid for four hours!" we say, looking absolutely outraged.

"Where is he? What did you do to him? We're calling the police!"

Cue panic on her face.

Then, just as she's about to have a mini heart attack, we burst out laughing.

Best. Prank. Ever.

MYKONOS MADE ME DO IT

"ONLY IN MYKONOS"

So, we're all sitting at breakfast the next morning, casually talking about the previous night at Porta—laughing, recounting the stories of a classic Mykonos mad night.

Then Mike pipes up,

"I did well, for anyone who did not notice. I was making out with this guy last night, no shirt, hairy chest, and his kiss tasted like... strawberry?"

Lisa freezes mid-bite, eyes wide.

"Wait. No shirt, hairy chest, and strawberry? Blond, curly hair?"

Mike squints, "Yeah, that's him. You saw us right? Were we too much?"

Lisa slowly puts her fork down, realizing the plot twist.

"No! I did not see you! I made out with him in the bathroom when I went to check my lipstic. You were with him too? He told me I was the only girl he fancied all night!"

And maybe she was.

They had both been making out with the same guy—the strawberry-scented, hairy-chested mystery man.

We all burst out laughing, and I'm just sitting there thinking, "Well, at least it wasn't a competition... or was it?"

MYKONOS MADE HIM DO IT

In July 2019, Mykonos got a scandal straight out of a Netflix script. Supermodels Gigi and Bella Hadid jetted in for a birthday trip—private villa, infinity pool, paparazzi in the bushes, the works. But instead of glamorous selfies, they got a break-in.

While the sisters were out celebrating, thieves slipped into their villa and cleaned the place out: jewellery, handbags, clothes, sunglasses—basically half of a Vogue shoot gone in minutes. When the Hadids came back, their bags had been dumped across the floor, valuables missing, and the party vibe instantly over.

The reaction? Gigi posted later on Instagram: "Don't let Insta fool you. Got robbed. Never going back lol. Wouldn't recommend. Spend your money elsewhere." That single line did more damage to Mykonos's image than any travel guide ever could. Imagine: one of the world's most photographed women telling her 50 million followers to avoid your island. Ouch.

But here's the twist: in the summer of 2025, Kylie Jenner (a close family friend of the Hadids) was spotted yacht-hopping around Mykonos. So while Gigi's vow to boycott still stands, Kylie came back. Mykonos, it seems, can't be cancelled.

The moral? No matter how rich, famous, or Instagram-ready you are, Mykonos can still rob you blind. Sometimes paradise comes with pickpockets.

"IT'S GONE"

We are at Moni.

DJ playing something between techno and a car alarm, and suddenly... a scream.

Not a casual scream. A drama school audition scream.

"MY EARRING! IT'S GONE! THE DIAMOND ONE!"

Instant chaos.

Music's still going, but the entire dancefloor turns into CSI: Mykonos.

iPhone flashlights are waving around like it's a Beyoncé concert.

Strangers are crawling, people on all fours, bartenders are squinting, even the DJ looks concerned.

Someone accuses the fog machine.

Someone else checks inside a shoe.

Someone yells, "CHECK HER HAIR!"

Another girl's like, "CHECK THE ICE BUCKET!"

It's chaos.

We are one step away from calling in Interpol .

Then—silence.

She freezes. Slowly reaches down her dress… and gasps.

"It's been in my boobs the whole time."

The crowd CHEERS.

A guy throws his hands up like we just scored a goal.

Someone does a shot in her honor.

I wipe away a tear and take a sip of my €42 vodka soda.

And then...

Her best friend—heels off, lashes unbothered—just looks at her, raises a hand, and slaps her.

Not hard. Just enough to say,

"Get a grip, Anastasia."

MYKONOS MADE HER DO IT

"IN DENIAL"

At 2:55AM, I made the classic Mykonos announcement:

"I'm just going outside to check if there are any taxis."

Translation: I'm done. I want to go home.

If there's a cab, I'm vanishing like a myth.

But outside? Nothing.

Just a few confused souls staring at the road like it owed them a ride.

So, I strutted back into the club like I'd been out for a refreshing breeze.

More dancing. More denial.

Repeat. Still no taxis.

More denial. More dancing.

By sunrise, I was less of a partygoer and more of a hostage.

I finally caught the first public bus into town, sunglasses on, surrounded by pensioners heading to church, holding my empty water bottle like a trophy from war.

And that's how I learned:

In Mykonos, you don't leave the party. The party releases you.

MYKONOS MADE ME DO IT

Scandal #4: The Archaeologist Beaten for Doing Her Job

In most places, an archaeologist is the person who gets excited over old stones and pots. In Mykonos, being an archaeologist can get you beaten up.

In 2023, a senior archaeologist responsible for supervising construction projects on the island was attacked outside her home. Why? Because she had the nerve to enforce the law and block illegal building works that threatened archaeological sites. The message from the attackers was clear: stop interfering with the construction frenzy that fuels Mykonos's luxury villa boom.

The story hit the front pages in Greece and even the international press. Le Monde described the island as being "in the crosshairs of Greek authorities," while Greek outlets openly talked about the "construction mafia" that treats Mykonos like a cash machine. Suddenly, the glamorous island of sunsets and champagne was also the island of bruised archaeologists and shadowy developers.

The scandal shocked Athens. Politicians promised crackdowns, inspections were ordered, and words like "lawlessness" and "corruption" started to appear in official speeches. For a moment, it felt like Mykonos might get cleaned up. But locals just rolled their eyes—they've seen it all before.

The moral? On this island, protecting history can be dangerous business. In Mykonos, even the ruins aren't safe from developers, and neither are the people trying to guard them.

"THE SANDCASTLE FOR SALE"

I was lying on the beach, minding my own SPF-50 business, when I saw this guy building a massive sandcastle—like, architectural digest level.

Towers, moat, a tiny driveway.

Then… he stuck a "FOR SALE" sign in front of it.

I thought, "Wow. Someone's deep into the vacation fantasy."

But nope—this was content.

Turns out, it was a TikTok prank, and the guy was filming how many people would seriously ask:

"How much is it?"

"Is it a time-share?"

"Does it come with the umbrella?"

I watched at least six people fall for it.

One even offered to Venmo a deposit.

At some point, he yelled:

"You break it, you buy it!"

…to a seagull.

I asked if I could move in.

He said sure, but only if I brought my own bucket.

MYKONOS MADE ME DO IT

"IS THIS A MUSEUM?"

My friend moved into a windmill in Mykonos for all the right reasons (see previous page). Little she knew.

By Day 3, she'd already given three accidental tours, accepted two €5 tips she didn't know how to refuse, and been asked if she also had a giftshop with souvenirs—twice.

One day, a man walked in with a GoPro and said, "Wow, this exhibit feels so real." She was brushing her teeth.

In desperation, she had to tape a sign to the door:

"NOT A MUSEUM. YES, I LIVE HERE. NO, YOU CAN'T COME IN."

It only made things worse. Now tourists line up to take selfies with the sign. She caught one couple posing with it, captioning their Instagram post:

"Authentic Greek experience. Locals live so simply."

Last week, she came home to a group of Americans asking if she offered guided tours in English.

She sighed, let them in, and said, "This way to the bedroom exhibit." She now charges €10.

MYKONOS MADE HER DO IT

Scandal #5: The 300-Person Villa Party

Mykonos has always been the island of "more." More champagne, more DJs, more people squeezed into a pool than physics should allow. But in 2022, one party finally had too much — and the police decided to RSVP.

It happened in a rented luxury villa, the kind with endless Instagram views and a price tag that could buy a small house on the mainland. Guests showed up in waves — by midnight, there were nearly 300 people crammed into the place. The music thundered, the drinks flowed, and the villa lit up like a nightclub. The only thing missing was a license.

When police raided the scene, they found not just partygoers, but also cash boxes, staff running bars without permits, and drugs tucked away between magnum bottles. The host and several employees were arrested, and the headlines the next day were pure tabloid heaven: "Mykonos Villa Turns Into Illegal Superclub."

Of course, this is Mykonos, so reactions were mixed. Some tourists complained the raid ruined the night. Locals rolled their eyes — as if this was the first time a villa had turned into Studio 54 with a swimming pool.

The moral? In Mykonos, private villas aren't just for quiet family holidays. Sometimes, they're the hottest clubs in town — until the police show up and kill the vibe.

"BOTH NEEDED"

I was at this chic little Mykonos restaurant, sipping rosé with a friend, when two stunning, fabulously dressed Black girls sat at the next table.

They had the kind of style that makes you feel underdressed in linen.

A tall, ridiculously handsome guy from another table stood up to go to the bathroom.

All of us looked. I mean — we *had* to.

One of the girls turns to me, dead serious:

"He's more into you than me."

I blinked. "Why?"

"Because he didn't even *look* at me. He's obviously gay."

We laughed and started chatting. She was magnetic — the kind of woman who could host a TED Talk on power dynamics and make it fashion.

She told me she had two boyfriends: One, an older banker she adored — smart, kind, generous.

"He really loves me," she said.

"And the second?" I asked.

"A club bouncer."

I raised an eyebrow. "But why, if the banker is all that?"

She leaned in, sipped her drink, and said:

"The banker's mind is full of meetings, markets, mortgages… The bouncer? When we're in bed, *he's present*. He has nothing else to think about."

And that's the day I realized — Mykonos has its own logic.

MYKONOS MADE ME DO IT

Mykonos isn't exactly shy about its chaos, but in the summer of 2025, things went next level. In broad daylight, right outside a busy restaurant, tourists and police ended up in a full-on street fight.

Videos shot by bystanders showed the scene: sunburned visitors squaring up against uniformed officers, shouting in three languages, plates crashing in the background, and smartphones everywhere capturing every punch. Within hours, the clips went viral — not exactly the island promo the Greek Tourism Ministry had in mind.

According to reports, it all started with a dispute over a bill. Voices got louder, tempers flared, and by the time the police arrived, nobody was in the mood for negotiation. The result? A messy brawl that looked more like a Saturday night bar fight than a civilized intervention by law enforcement.

The moral? On this island, even lunch can turn into WrestleMania. And if you do get into an argument with the police, just remember: in Mykonos, the crowd is always ready to film — and upload.

"THAT'S NOT YOUR TOWEL, SIR"

I left my towel on the sunbed, ran into the sea like I was in a perfume ad. Ten minutes later, I come back—some guy is sitting on my sunbed.

Naked. On my black think velvet towel. Legs spread like he paid extra for the breeze. He smiles like we're old friends.

"Oh! Sorry I thought this was one of the towels the beach gives out. And the bed was free!" Right. Free towel. Free sunbed. Free d*** show. The beach was full, so I sat on the sunbed next to him.

Like this was normal.

I bought a new towel because mine was now… spiritually unclean. And every time he talked to me, I had to look slightly over his head like I was watching imaginary seagulls.

I spent the next hour nodding politely while carefully maintaining eye contact—because the man was hugely blessed and had zero shame. Kinda understandable.

We covered politics, the price of sardines, and the best souvlaki in town—while I never once looked below the collarbone.

When he left, he patted my shoulder and said, "Thanks for being chill." I nodded, still not blinking.

I'm not chill. I'm just Greek. We suffer in silence.

I left the towel on the sunbed for the next naked customer.

MYKONOS MADE ME DO IT

67

"THE SUNBED COIN TOSS"

Found the last free sunbed at the beach club—felt like I'd won the lottery without buying a ticket.

Just as I was about to claim it, a group of tourists spotted it too, marching over like it was the last lifeboat on the Titanic.

We all stood there, awkwardly polite, aggressively passive.

I smiled, pulled a coin from my bag (yes, I came prepared), and said, "Let's flip for it."

They blinked. "Is this… normal?"

"Only in Mykonos," I said, channelling my inner game show host.

I called heads. Flipped. It landed on heads. Obviously.

I nodded solemnly like Zeus had spoken. Sat down. Victory sip.

One of them laughed, "We'll bring a coin next time."

Another muttered, "Or a reservation."

Then—get this—the waitress came over and said, "Sorry, these are reserved."

We got drunk together at the bar. Like civilized animals.

MYKONOS MADE ME DO IT

Scandal #7: The €125,000 Champagne Bottle

If you thought €500 for a sunbed was bad, welcome to Psarou Beach—home of the most expensive bottle of champagne in Greece. At Mykonos's most famous beach club, popping a cork can cost you as much as €125,000. Some reports even whisper about €140,000 for certain rare bottles.

The "bottle" in question isn't your average Dom Pérignon. We're talking about collector-sized, ultra-rare formats—the kind of thing that looks more like a fire extinguisher than a drink. Order one, and it doesn't just arrive at your table. It arrives with sparklers, security guards, a small parade of staff, and half the beach watching you like you just won the lottery.

And that's the point. Nobody buys these bottles for the taste. They buy them for the spectacle—the show of power, money, and "look at me" energy that Mykonos thrives on. For the price of a villa deposit, you get ten minutes of pure attention and a champagne shower that Instagram will never forget.

Of course, the tax inspectors eventually noticed. Between fines, raids, and unpaid millions, the champagne scandals at Psarou became as famous as the parties themselves. But by then, the image was set: Mykonos wasn't just an island. It was the world's most glamorous receipt.

The moral? In Mykonos, some people don't just drink champagne—they weaponize it. And if you can drop €125,000 on bubbles, you're not buying alcohol. You're buying immortality, one Instagram story at a time.

"THE CHAMPAGNE SHOWER INCIDENT"

It was a classic Mykonos beach day: sunbeds packed, music loud, everyone pretending they weren't checking themselves out in their sunglasses.

Then suddenly—like a siren call—I heard it.

"CHAMPAGNE SHOWER!"

A shirtless guy stood on his lounger like Zeus, holding a bottle of Dom Pérignon over his head, shaking it like it owed him money.

The cork exploded. The foam followed.

But instead of raining bubbly glory on his friend group, the champagne took a sharp left...

And landed directly on a poor woman reading her Kindle.

She didn't even look up.

She just wiped her screen, turned the page, and muttered,

"Tell Jeff Bezos I want a refund."

The guy shouted, "Sorry! My bad!"

She replied: "Only if you refill my prosecco."

They ended up drinking together.

I think they're dating now.

Or suing each other. Hard to tell in Mykonos.

MYKONOS MADE THEM DO IT.

"WAITER COME HERE PLEASE"

We're on our second bottle of wine at Nammos, feeling like Psarou royalty. Dancing on the chairs thanx to great music and a wine which is divine. Crisp, cold, fruity.

An hour later, I am having the time of my life. I'm dancing, hair in full Beyoncé mode, glass in hand. I sip with lust and immediately stop like someone just cut the music.

"Hold up—this wine is wrong. Abort."

I tell everyone. The team investigation starts.

We pour. We sip. We pause.

"Yes... this isn't the same."

We compare it to the tiny drop left in the first glass like we're judges on MasterChef.

It's definitely different. Dryer, woodier, more complex.

So we do what any normal, well-behaved table at Nammos would do: we start a scene.

Call the waiter. Explain the scandal.

Accuse. Point. Whisper dramatically.

Ask to speak to the sommelier (we don't know what that is, but it sounds powerful).

The staff looks confused.

Tension is high. Until...

A woman at the next table, in Chanel sunglasses and emotional exhaustion, leans over and says:

"I think you drank our wine."

Turns out, the bottle holders were right next to each other — we grabbed theirs.

Plus we never ordered a 3rd bottle after ours finished. We'd been swirling, judging, and trash-talking their €300 bottle like it was a fraud.

Silence.

Then... nervous laughter. Awkward toasts.

One of us said, "Well at least it was a good vintage."

We got our actual bottle, but by then, the wine didn't taste the same. It tasted like shame.

MYKONOS MADE ME DO IT

Scandal #8: The €20 Cruise Passenger Fee

In 2025, the Greek government finally admitted what everyone in Mykonos already knew: cruise ships were sinking the island, not the other way around. With around 900 ships a year unloading 1.5 million passengers, the whitewashed alleys turned into human traffic jams and the trash piled up faster than the cocktails.

So they introduced a new rule: every cruise passenger pays €20 to set foot on Mykonos. The money, they promised, would go to infrastructure, cleaning, and restoring some balance.

On paper, it sounded like progress. For locals, cruise passengers were never big spenders anyway. They buy a fridge magnet, snap a selfie by the windmills, maybe eat a gyro, and then rush back to the ship before sunset. In return, the island gets noise, litter, and gridlock. As one Mykonian shopkeeper put it: "They bring us headaches, not euros."

But not everyone cheered. Tour companies complained it was unfair, some tourists cried "cash grab," and the international press painted it as a war on cruise travel.

The truth lies somewhere in the middle. Yes, the €20 fee might help keep the island afloat. But it also put Mykonos on the global map as a place that literally charges you just to set foot on it. For an island already seen as the poster child of over-the-top pricing, the optics weren't great.

The moral? In Mykonos, even stepping ashore comes at a cost. And if you arrive on a floating city of 5,000 passengers, if you're bringing the party, bring your wallet too.

"BILL SPLIT"

Guy 1: "Okay, my pasta was €19. I'll add €2 for the water."

Girl 1: "We all drank the water."

Guy 1: "Yeah, but I poured it."

Girl 2: "I didn't drink it. I'm doing that thing where I only hydrate with cucumber."

Guy 2: "Wait, did we include the cover charge? What even is a cover charge? We didn't see a show."

Girl 3: "I only ate fries."

Guy 1: "You ate half my tzatziki."

Girl 3: "It was communal."

Guy 2: "Let's just split evenly."

Girl 1: "I didn't have wine."

Girl 2: "I didn't have dairy."

Guy 1: "I didn't have fun." (silence)

Girl 3: "Guys… the waiter's watching us like we're planning a heist."

Waiter: "Would you like the bill split six ways?"

All: "NO."

MYKONOS MADE THEM DO IT

CRUISE TOURISTS ANECDOTES

I have this friend who is a waiter at one of the popular fish taverns at the port, where they get lots of visitors from the cruises. The other day he told me just a few of the things he remembered from his weird encounters with this specific type of customer, the cruise tourist.

The Onion-Free Negotiator

Customer: "What's the price of a gyro without onions?" Waiter: "The same." Customer: "Even with no onions?"

The Vegan Feta Question

Customer: "Is feta vegan?" Waiter: "The goat it came from was vegan indeed."

The Waiting Room

Customer: "We don't want to eat, we just want to sit here until the boat comes."

Waiter: "Great! I'll bring you complimentary boredom."

The Coke Light Crisis

Customer: "Do you have Diet Coke?"

Waiter: "We have Coke Light."

Customer: "No thanks, we want Diet."

Waiter: "Same soda, different disappointment."

The Beer Quartet

Customer: "We'll just have one beer, please."

Waiter: "Sure."

Customer: "Also bring four glasses. We'll share."

Waiter returned with four tiny shot glasses. Nobody blinked.

The Greek Salad Trio

Customer: "We'll have just one Greek salad."

Waiter: "Okay."

Customer: "And three forks." They dissected the feta like surgeons in silence.

Tap Water Warriors

Customer: "We'll have tap water, please."

Waiter: "It's not potable."

Customer: "We'll risk it. We survived Egypt."

Cruise Alarm Clock

Customer 1: "We'll just have a Coke each."

Customer 2: "And what is it now? 1pm? Well, please bring the bill at 3:40 — our boat leaves at 4."

Waiter: "Sure. Would you like a gentle wake-up call or something with drums?"

Moussaka Confusion

Customer: "What's in the moussaka?"

Waiter: "Eggplant, meat, béchamel..."

Customer: "So it's like lasagna?"

Waiter: "If lasagna studied abroad."

In 2018, Lindsay Lohan decided Mykonos needed more than sunbeds and champagne. It needed her. The actress opened her very own beach club on Kalo Livadi, complete with orange sun loungers, VIP cabanas, and MTV cameras ready to turn it into a reality show: Lindsay Lohan's Beach Club.

The hype was unreal. This wasn't just another Mykonos hot spot — this was a comeback story. Lindsay, reborn as a businesswoman, dancing barefoot on the sand, welcoming guests like a Greek goddess of nightlife. For a few weeks, it looked like she'd cracked the Mykonos code.

But then… it all unravelled. Staff complained of chaos, bills went unpaid, and the MTV series turned into unintentional comedy — more about drama among the employees than any glamorous celebrity rebirth. By the following summer, the club was shuttered, the loungers gone, and the site returned quietly to the island's long list of "one-season wonders."

Tabloids called it a "Greek tragedy." Locals called it predictable. Mykonos has seen countless dreamers arrive with stars in their eyes and leave with empty wallets. Lindsay's only mistake was doing it on camera.

The moral? In Mykonos, even celebrities learn the hard way: the island always wins. Lohan Beach Club is still there, but not Lindsay.

"ON FIRE BUT FIRED"

A friend of mine visiting from Athens had his life dream to go to Scorpios. And he dressed the part: linen pants, flowing linen shirt, leather sandals, all earthy colors, fitting seamlessly to the Scorpios decor — but also sporting the official staff uniform.

And that was his dream night: Within minutes, a group of influencers asked him for a bottle of rosé and truffle fries.

Somehow by the end of the night, he'd earned €40 in tips and two phone numbers.

Every five minutes, someone waved him down.

One guy asked for the bill.

Another handed him their Amex.

A girl followed him to the bar and asked if he could get her the "staff discount." He said yes, took her order, and brought her drink — from our bottle. She gave him a €20 billl and called him "an angel."

By the end of the night, he was fully committed. Clearing glasses, high-fiving the DJ, emptying ashtrays — even the real staff started nodding at him like he belonged.

Then, someone reported him for not actually doing his job.

And that was the reason we had to leave — in shame — for our incompetent friend who had managed to get fired from a job he never had.

MYKONOS MADE HIM DO IT

In Mykonos, it's not just cocktails and champagne that cost a fortune — sometimes it's the fines. In 2023, a local businessman was slapped with a jaw-dropping €955,000 penalty after authorities discovered he had failed to declare 199 villas that he was renting out short-term.

The scheme was simple: the villas were managed and rented through platforms, but never registered in the official property system. For each undeclared villa, the fine was €5,000. Multiply that by 199 and you don't get a luxury shopping spree — you get a scandal almost worth a million euros.

The case became a symbol of Mykonos's shadow economy. On an island where villas change hands faster than beach club cocktails, the temptation to skip paperwork — and taxes — is strong. Everyone wants a slice of the tourist gold rush, but not everyone wants to share it with the taxman. That was a turning point: since then, controls have tightened and inspections are more frequent.

The moral? In Mykonos, villas aren't just luxury escapes — they're also prime scandal material. And while you can hide the paperwork, you can't hide from the taxman forever.

"BOOKED: ENTIRE PLACE (TERMS APPLY)"

Okay, so I booked this "entire place" on Airbnb, thinking it was my own private Cycladic paradise. The pictures showed a secluded terrace, perfect for some uninterrupted sun soaking.

Day two, I'm living my best nudist life, sprawled out like a starfish, soaking up the Greek rays. Pure bliss. Suddenly, the door creaks open, and there stands a very tanned, very surprised gentleman holding a basket of laundry.

Turns out, "entire place" apparently meant "entire guest place," and the owner, Nikos, lived just downstairs. His eyes widened, I yelped and scrambled for a towel that felt approximately the size of a postage stamp. The silence was so thick, you could spread it on toast.

Nikos, bless his soul, just chuckled, mumbled something about "beautiful tan lines," and backed away slowly.

For the rest of the trip, we communicated mostly through nervous nods and baked goods left at the door. Every time I heard a creak, I threw on a towel like it was the Met Gala.

My private paradise had a very friendly, and slightly traumatized, landlord.

MYKONOS MADE ME DO IT

MYKONOS FAQs

This isn't the part of the book where I tell you where to party or where to see and be seen. For that, check the eBook version — it's packed with Top 10s, survival tips, and the practical stuff you'll actually use on the ground.

Here, we're tackling a different kind of question: the ones that pop up on Google autocomplete, the ones people ask me mostly when I'm not in Mykonos, and the ones you wonder about before you even decide to book a ticket.

These answers come from 35 years of loving and living Mykonos. They're totally hands-on, honest, and sometimes controversial.

Others might disagree with me — and that's fine. Most of these topics have fuelled endless debates among locals and loyals for the last five years anyway.

FAQ #1: Is Mykonos worth visiting?

Short answer: yes. Long answer: absolutely yes. But don't just take my word for it — that's why I created the eBook version of this guide. It's packed with proof: photos, Top 10 lists, and detailed tips that show you exactly *why* Mykonos is unlike anywhere else.

Here, let me give you just five of the strongest reasons:

1. **The Beauty:** The whitewashed houses, the narrow alleys, the light, the sea, the sunsets — it's a unique place in the world, and it looks like nowhere else.

2. **The Beaches:** Mykonos has some of the best beaches in the world. Period.

3. **The Parties:** The island wrote the manual on day-to-night parties. No one else does it on this level — not even Ibiza.

4. **The Energy:** Mykonos has a magnetic vibe — a mix of freedom, chaos, glamour, and mischief. It's not just a place, it's a feeling.

5. **The People-Watching:** Where else can you see billionaires, global celebrities, influencers, and me all in one square kilometer? If they keep coming back, they can't all be wrong.

And let's be clear: this isn't some passing fad. Mykonos has been a top desired destination for over 80 years, drawing Hollywood stars in the 1950s, jet-setters in the 1980s, and Instagrammers today. Trends change, but the island's pull never fades.

The truth is: Mykonos is like New York City — you might love it or hate it, but you'll still want to go just to see it for yourself.

"SHOW"

We were halfway through our eggs benedict when Andreas stood up on the terrace like he was about to accept a Nobel Prize.

Arms raised, sunglasses slightly crooked, and with a mimosa in one hand, he shouted:

"I JUST WANT TO SAY—I LOVE THIS ISLAND!"

Forks paused. Heads turned. A baby cried.

I immediately looked down at my plate, hoping the table would swallow me whole.

The waiter sighed. A German tourist clapped.

Andreas, now drunk on attention (and also four mimosas), spread his arms wider like Moses parting the brunch crowd.

"THE ENERGY HERE? IMMACULATE!"

He knocked over our water carafe mid-declaration. The table was soaked. My phone took a hit.

I leaned in and whispered,

"Bro, for real? After yesterday? After pushing your scooter uphill at Super?"

He blinked but kept going.

"And the bee bite? Your allergy could have killed you."

He winced but nodded.

"Plus the AirPod you lost into the drain. You spent an hour fishing it out with a souvlaki stick."

At this point, he sighed, took another mimosa sip, and said: "don't you see it?"

See what? That your life sucks here?

"That since I arrived I am the center of attention on this island. Only here could my disasters turn into a show."

Teo appeared silently and handed me the bill without making eye contact. Time to go... before another show... of bad luck.

MYKONOS MADE HIM DO IT

FAQ #2: Is Mykonos really that expensive?

Yes, it is. But let's be fair: Greece overall has gotten more expensive overall. Mykonos just takes it one step further.

What's really expensive?

- The flights from Athens to Mykonos — you're in the air for just 20 minutes, yet the ticket often costs more than your international flight into Athens.

- The beaches. A sunbed "set" now averages over €100, with an additional minimum consumption on top.

- The hot spots. If you want to see and be seen where the celebrities are, you'll pay outrageous prices. But that's true in Saint-Tropez, Ibiza, or Miami too.

Everything else — hotels, drinks, food, transportation — exists on a sliding scale. You can find reasonable options, and you can find ridiculous ones. The choice is yours. Can you survive on a budget? Yes. Here's how it looks:

- Airbnb or a "room to let" somewhere in the middle of nowhere.

- Local restaurants and fast food spots with normal prices.

- Public buses and the occasional local taxi (avoid private transfers if you can).

- Drinks in Chora (the town) for around €10.

- And, most importantly: pick the right month. July and August are insane. In June or September you'll save money *and* sanity.

"YOU ARE WAY OVER, DUDE"

"I want the cheapest sunbed you have but with shade".

I was very honest and precise with the gentleman responsible for the sunbeds.

"Are you alone? If so, it is 50 for the sunbed with a minimum consumption of 70EURO. That's all I can offer at this point, we are full." He was also honest and precise.

That is 120 EURO for 2-3 hours at the beach. Be it. You only live once.

90 minutes later, the same gentleman comes to me and drops this:

"When I told you about the minimum consumption of 70EURO, you said that it is too much for a couple of hours at the beach at 4pm. I just want to inform you that your bill stands currently at 210EURO already. We had a laugh about this with your waiter".

Yes, they did. He was still laughing.

Well I had met the Italian couple from the sunbeds next to me and the bottles of prosecco were popping faster than New Year's eve fireworks. Dancing, laughing, prosecco, dancing, laughing, prosecco and not always with this order.

Ah, I forgot, I also got some sushi.

MYKONOS MADE ME DO IT

"OH NO"

So, I've got these ridiculously rich friends from Cyprus. You know the type—come to Mykonos for four days and casually drop a million like they're buying gum.

Naturally, they hit the classics: Skorpios, Nammos, Interni, Zuma. But they don't just go—they go full Roman Emperor. We're talking €500 sunbeds, €1,000 wine like it's tap water, the works.

Now, they're lovely people, truly. But their idea of "grabbing a bite" is my idea of refinancing my future.

So I start ducking invites. "Oh nooo, I've got a... windmill emergency?" I dodge three outings until finally I get the message:

"Tonight. Dinner. Cavo Tagoo. No excuses."

Okay, fine. I psych myself up for what I tell myself will be a "manageable" €200 dinner.

I breathe in, breathe out, and show up.

Cocktails first—obviously. Then it's time to order food.

They go for fish. Not just a fish. Fish by the kilo. Fish that costs more per gram than gold.

They choose lavraki and want it prepared four different ways. Like, who knew fish could do Cirque du Soleil?

I panic. I'm not trying to auction off a kidney tonight.

So I make a calculated, budget-conscious move:

"I'll just have the... uh, seabass. I don't like lavraki."

Silence.

The waiter pauses.

Then, with the gentleness of someone announcing a terminal diagnosis: "Sir… seabass is lavraki."

My friends are silent.

I'm silent.

The lavraki is silent—probably judging me from the kitchen.

Anyway, I ate my shame. With a side of truffle mashed potatoes.

MYKONOS MADE ME DO IT

FAQ #3: When should I go to Mykonos?

If you've been dreaming of Mykonos in July and August — don't. Those months may be peak season, but they're also peak madness: overcrowded, overpriced, and overheated.

The sweet spots? May, early June, September, and even October. And here's why:

- **The weather:** Greece shines in these months. You still get sunshine and swimming, but without the suffocating heatwaves.

- **The service:** At the beginning of summer, both locals and Seasonistas are still fresh and excited. You feel the difference when your waiter actually smiles because he isn't on his 90th shift in a row.

- **The prices:** They crank up on July 1st and drop back down on September 1st. Timing your trip literally saves you hundreds.

- **The quality of tourism:** You'll meet people with better wallets, better attitudes, and better energy. Translation: fewer show-offs, more actual fun.

- **The vibe:** In the off-season, you meet people who came for the island's beauty — not just for a post. The conversations are better, the sunsets feel more real.

- **The celebrities:** The *real* ones avoid the crowds. If you're hoping for a surprise encounter, it's more likely in May or September than in the circus of August.

"MASSAGE BY MISTAKE"

I was napping on a sunbed in Mykonos, face-down, towel over my head, totally gone—dreaming of saganaki and shirtless waiters.

Suddenly, I felt heaven. Hands. Oils. Magic.

I thought, "Wow. Mykonos really knows how to deliver."

Strong but gentle. Like a Greek grandma kneading dough, but spiritually.

I let it happen. I didn't ask questions.

Fifteen minutes in, I finally stirred, lifted my head, and turned slightly to thank whoever arranged this divine intervention.

That's when the masseuse gasped, took two steps back and said:

"You're not Mr. Stefano!"

Apparently, she was booked for the guy on the next bed.

Who, by the way, was wide awake watching us the whole time, mouthing: "Bro... what?!"

I offered to switch places, but the damage (and knots) were done.

She gave me a business card and told me to "you book properly next time."

I tipped her in feta.

MYKONOS MADE ME DO IT

FAQ #4: Is Mykonos safe?

Yes — very. In fact, Mykonos is one of the safest places in the Mediterranean, and even more so for solo female travelers. Crime rates are low, violent incidents are rare, and the island lives off tourism, so safety is non-negotiable.

I can tell you this from experience: I've been here for **35 summers**, often out until 9 a.m., and nothing has *ever, ever* happened to me. There has never been an incident against women. There are people everywhere at all times — on the streets, in the clubs, at the beaches — and that presence alone adds another layer of safety.

That said, Mykonos isn't a bubble. Petty theft can happen (especially in clubs or on busy beaches). But petty crime hasn't stopped you from visiting Paris, London, or Barcelona, and it shouldn't stop you from coming here either.

Now, if you're male, have had nine beers, and decide to pick a fight, that's a different story — but honestly, that could just as easily happen at your local pub back home.

The truth? For women traveling alone, Mykonos is remarkably safe. The nightlife is lively without being predatory, the streets are full of people until late, and locals are used to independent travelers. Use a bit of common sense and you'll feel secure and free to enjoy yourself.

You'll probably feel safer walking around Mykonos at 2 a.m. than in many big European cities. It's safe, it's fun, and it lets you relax — the only thing really at risk is your bank account.

"I ALMOST IMPRESSED ME"

"It's 2pm. Are you any close to be ready for hitting the beach?" asks my friend, when I answered finally her 17th call.

"Not really, I just opened my Mediterranean brown eyes. I feel OK, so I will be ready in 30. Wait. Question. Why don't I feel hungry? Normally I feel so hungry when I wake up. Plus I do not see any food laying around. Did I reach the point that I can live solely on alcohol? No food required anymore in Mykonos?"

I almost impressed me for a moment.

"No" was her definite and abrupt answer. "No you still depend on food, sorry. You ate at Jimmy's in the morning before going to bed. I bought it for you, I paid for it and you ate right there with Jimmy himself. Don't you remember?"

I was honest. No, I remembered nothing.

"Not even the bleach?" she asked.

The bleach? Which bleach?

"They had just mopped the floor with bleach and because I was wearing long pants, I did not go in, not to ruin it. I ordered and paid from outside. You found that very funny and you couldn't stop giggling. Any recollection of all this?".

Nope, natha.

MYKONOS MADE ME DO IT

"THE FEET WERE NOT FREE"

I was sunbathing peacefully when a woman walked by, stopped, and stared at my feet.

Not my face.

Not my tan.

Just. My. Feet.

She looked up and asked,

"Do you do OnlyFans?"

I laughed, thinking it was a joke.

It wasn't.

She was a real foot content creator and said my toes had "great symmetry" (never heard that before).

She begged to take one photo—"Just for inspiration."

Next thing I know, I'm the cover photo on her "Summer Toes in Mykonos" post.

I didn't get paid.

But the comment section was wild.

One guy wrote: "I'd drink ouzo from those."

Now I wear socks to the beach.

                                    MYKONOS MADE ME DO IT

FAQ #5: Mykonos or Santorini?

Ah, the eternal question. People ask it like you have to choose between them — but the truth is, Mykonos and Santorini are two completely different planets sharing the same sea.

Santorini is drama. The cliffside caldera, the blue-domed churches, the volcanic beaches, and those sunsets people actually clap for. It's couples, honeymooners, photographers, and anyone who wants their Instagram to look like a glossy travel magazine. It's breathtaking, romantic, and sometimes overwhelming.

Mykonos is pure pulse. Days drift into nights, nights spill into mornings, and the beaches beat like open-air dance floors. The island throws everyone together into one restless, glittering mix. It's where glamour collides with freedom, and where mischief always has an invitation.

So which one is "better"?

- If you want romance, views, wine, and history → Santorini.

- If you want beaches, nightlife, people-watching, and pure vibe → Mykonos.

And if you want me to decide for you — and trust me, I'll be objective — here's my take: if you're with your friends, definitely go to Mykonos. If you're with your significant other, start with Santorini… and when you've had your fill of romance (or you're bored), come over to Mykonos for the real fun.

The truth? Santorini is the postcard you frame. Mykonos is the chapter you write.

"MEET ME AT REMEZZO"

"Meet me at Remezzo at 7.30pm for the sunset" I said with confidence. She agreed, although I sensed some doubt even through the phone.

4 hours later, I am enjoying a Porn Star by myself, as often people do with porn stars.

At 7.30pm exactly, I see my phone blinking.

"Where are you?" she is asking me with her usual happy energy.

"I am on time, girl, waiting for you".

"I do not see you", she burst into laughs.

"Well it is crowded, I am here, by the door, wait I just saw Kostas, I need to say hi" and I hang up.

5 minutes later, the phone blinks again and I get the "where are you" again!

"For real now? I told you by the door!".

She said that she checked all doors and she cannot find me.

And the interrogation starts. The usual interrogation when one is lost in Mykonos: "what do you see?". I started describing the people around me. Nope, that was not helpful.

"Girl I am sitting right under the sign that says Caprice, why can't you see me?"

That helped tons.

Both of us.

"ARE YOU KIDDING ME? YOU SAID REMEZZO" she screamed still laughing.

20 minutes later, she was standing in front me, asking me if I was taking revenge for something she did and if I sent her on purpose to the other side of the very busy Chora in August.

The truth was that till that moment I was convinced that I was at Remezzo. The familiarity of both places over the years, plus the alcohol of the night before seem the only viable explanation.

It was not on purpose.

MYKONOS MADE ME DO IT

FAQ #6: Mykonos or Ibiza?

They get compared all the time — and for good reason. Both are about music, DJs, beach parties, celebrities, and outrageous prices. But scratch the surface and you'll see they're very different experiences.

Where Mykonos beats Ibiza:

- **The beaches:** Mykonos wins hands down with golden sand, turquoise water, and from hidden coves to all-day party spots.

- **The old town (Chora):** A maze of whitewashed alleys, bars, and boutiques — Ibiza has much less like it.

- **The island feel:** Mykonos is compact, minimal, glamorous and pure Cycladic charm. No highways, no sprawl.

- **History & culture:** Delos, a UNESCO World Heritage site and one of the great archaeological treasures of the Mediterranean.

Where Ibiza beats Mykonos:

- **The calendar:** Ibiza runs year-round — even Christmas. Mykonos is strictly May to October.

- **Accessibility:** Ibiza has far more flights, from everywhere.

- **The landscape:** Ibiza is greener, with forests and hills.

A weekend in Ibiza works. But in Mykonos, you'll want a week to really settle into the rhythm of beaches, Chora, and endless nights.

The truth? Ibiza is always on. Mykonos is a summer fling — but one you'll never forget.

"WTF"

I met my friends at a bar before hitting the clubs.

I was feeling myself — strong dark blue fitted blazer, just bought that day on mega sale. Dead cheap, but it looked expensive, and my friends loved it.

We head to the club. Our table is right by the dancefloor. The place is packed.

I meet someone. Sparks. We leave together before anyone else. Let's just say... 10/10 night.

Next morning, hungover. Barely awake. Flying back in 3 hours.

My friend calls — she's furious. Her expensive black blazer is gone. She searched everywhere, even called the club. Nada. She's gutted. Says someone must've taken it and left a cheap one behind, but she refused to bring that thing home.

I sympathize, hang up, start packing. And then…

There it is. A black blazer. Not mine.

HER. JACKET. Yep. I took hers.

And the cheap one? The one she refused to take home? Was mine.

The one she helped me put on before I left with my mystery date. We laughed for days. I did go back looking for my beloved blazer.

Gone forever.

MYKONOS MADE ME DO IT

FAQ #7: Why is Mykonos white?

Because it's iconic — but also because it was practical. The whitewashed houses of Mykonos weren't designed as Instagram backdrops; they were built for survival.

- **Heat:** White reflects the sun, keeping interiors cooler during brutal Greek summers.

- **Limewash:** Traditionally, homes were coated with lime, which was cheap, abundant, and had antibacterial properties. It even helped fight cholera outbreaks in the 1930s.

- **Uniformity:** In the 1960s, the Greek government passed regulations requiring Cycladic islands to maintain the white-and-blue look. What started as practicality became cultural branding.

- **Aesthetic:** The result is one of the most recognizable island images in the world — narrow alleys of white cubes glowing against the Aegean blue.

So yes, Mykonos is white because of climate, health, and history. But also because once the world fell in love with the look, the island never dared to change it.

The truth? White wasn't chosen for Instagram. But it made Instagram possible.

"NOT MY BUDDHA BAR"

Booked Buddha-Bar weeks in advance, felt like a planning king.

Got dressed to stun — glowing like I was about to dine with royalty. Arrived in Mykonos ready for my reservation… only to be told it didn't exist.

Naturally, I argued. Gestured at my phone. Demanded they "check again."

Right in the middle of my Oscar-worthy meltdown, I got a ping — a cheerful SMS confirming my table for two… in Paris.

I froze. Smiled. Pretended it was a text from my agent.

Then waltzed past the host like I belonged there and found a seat at the bar, where a kind German couple immediately took me in.

We bonded over travel fails and shared a bottle of rosé they hadn't planned on sharing.

They spent most of the evening calmly explaining that the Greek economy was doing "much better than expected," because apparently they'd arrived expecting street beggars, not €25 cocktails and a champagne menu longer than the Constitution.

I nodded like I was the Minister of Finance and had personally balanced the budget. Snapped a flattering photo under the lanterns and posted:

"Buddha-Bar magic - always worth the wait #MykonosNights"

Technically, I wasn't lying.

I was at a Buddha-Bar. Just not my Buddha-Bar.

MYKONOS MADE ME DO IT

FAQ #8: Is Mykonos always windy?

Pretty much — yes. Mykonos didn't get the nickname *"The Island of the Winds"* by accident.

Why it's windy:

- In summer, the Meltemi winds blow down from the north, across the Aegean, caused by high-pressure systems over the Balkans clashing with low-pressure systems over Turkey.

- The result? A strong, dry, northerly wind that funnels right through the Cyclades — and Mykonos sits directly in its path, like a perfectly placed wind tunnel.

- The Meltemi can last for days, sometimes weeks, and it's strongest in July and August.

The upside:

The wind cools the island when the sun is brutal, clears the sky for those insane sunsets, and makes Mykonos heaven for windsurfers and sailors.

The downside:

It also means flying hats, collapsing beach umbrellas, and the occasional mojito blown straight into your lap.

So yes, Mykonos is windy — not hurricane windy, but consistently breezy.

The truth? The wind is part of Mykonos's DNA. It shaped the architecture (think windmills, narrow alleys), it decides which beaches you'll visit, and it's the island's natural air-conditioning. Without it, Mykonos would feel like an oven.

"HEN PARTY OR HELL PARTY?"

I was minding my business at the beach bar when I noticed a group of women in pink wigs and glittery swimsuits chanting something that sounded suspiciously like "freedom."

Naturally, I wandered over. One handed me a shot, another slapped a *"FINALLY HAPPY"* temporary tattoo onto my neck before I could object.

I assumed it was a wild hen party. I was wrong.

We ended up dancing in a circle like lunatics, sand flying, drinks spilling. At some point, the "bride" — or so I thought — shouts,

"This is what happiness smells like!" and hurls a ring into the sea like it's cursed.

Everyone cheers.

I nervously clap along, whispering to a bridesmaid,

"That's not... the engagement ring, right?"

She smirks: "Sweetie, that ring paid for this trip."

Still oblivious, I'm handed a Post-it and told to write a message "to the groom."

I scribble, "All the best!" and toss it into a small bonfire they built in a bucket.

Another woman yells, "Hope you marry your mother!"

Someone is burning a doll.

I realize I've been drafted into a **divorce party.**

The night ends with me leading a conga line around a very confused couple celebrating their honeymoon.

I still have the neck tattoo. And emotional damage.

MYKONOS MADE HER DO IT

FAQ #9: Is Mykonos gay?

Yes — and proudly so. Mykonos has been one of the world's top gay destinations since the 1970s. Long before Pride parades became mainstream, this little Cycladic island opened its arms to everyone.

Mykonos is gay-friendly:

- **History:** In the '70s and '80s, when Greece was still conservative, Mykonos quietly became a haven where people could be free. Jackie O's visit put it on the map, and the gay community made it glamorous.

- **Bars & clubs:** The island is packed with LGBTQ+ bars, drag shows, beach parties, and clubs — from Jackie O's to Babylon — that rival anywhere in the world.

- **The vibe:** It's not just about venues. The entire island runs on acceptance. Straight, gay, trans, bi, queer — no one blinks. Everyone is part of the same party.

- **Tourism DNA:** Gay travelers were pioneers here, shaping Mykonos into the cosmopolitan playground it is today. The luxury, the nightlife, the open-mindedness — much of it started with them.

But here's the update:

Mykonos is still gay-friendly, but it's *less gay* than before. Globally, gay people don't feel the same need for dedicated bars — they're just as comfortable in "mainstream" spots, and Mykonos reflects that shift.

There are fewer explicitly gay bars now. The rainbow is everywhere, but the spaces are more integrated.

The bigger issue? Mykonos is very expensive. Younger gay travellers often can't afford it, so the crowd skews older. Many gay venues today are filled with men over 50 — either looking at each other or at the younger rent boys who fly in from London, Paris, or Brazil for summer "work."

And this isn't just about the gay scene. The same pattern applies to straight Mykonos — and to every luxury destination in the world. When a place gets expensive, the crowd ages up, the younger people drop out, and the escort scene (male and female) fills the gap.

The truth? Mykonos isn't "gay-friendly." It's simply friendly. The rainbow has been flying here for 50 years, and it isn't coming down — but the scene has evolved. Today it's less about dedicated spaces, more about freedom everywhere. And money.

"FOR REEAL?!?!?! YES FOR REAL"

So I'm at this club in Mykonos, minding my own overpriced drink, dancing to music I pretend to like, when this guy slides over.

Tall, tanned, and tragically confident. Let's call him... Adonis.

We start chatting, and while dancing we cover the basics "where are you from?", "first time here", "what do you do for living" and "do you believe in soulmates?".

One hour later we have really hit it off, therefore he hits me with:

"How old are you?"

I smile and tell him. My real age. No filters, no rounding down, no astrology-based guesswork.

He blinks. "No no, really. How old are you?"

Okay. Weird, but fine. I say it again. I even throw in the birth year to help him do the math.

His eyes narrow like I just told him I was 400 years old and part of the furniture.

"You don't have to lie. Just say you're not interested."

Wait—what?

He thinks I'm lying about my age as a way to get rid of him. As if I'm running some elaborate psychological operation instead of just telling the truth.

So now I'm stuck in this weird standoff where I'm defending my birth certificate to a stranger in sunglasses indoors at midnight.

I say it again. Calmly.

He looks personally offended—like my actual age just slapped his ego across the face. He gets heated. Like really heated. I'm genuinely wondering if I'm about to be the first person in Mykonos history to start a fight with honesty.

Luckily, one of his friends steps in with a "bro, let it go" vibe, and I make a dramatic exit, sipping my €28 cocktail like it's tea.

Moral of the story?

In Mykonos, telling the truth might be the most dangerous thing you do all night.

MYKONOS MADE ME DO IT

"THE ACCIDENTAL BEACH TATTOO"

I fell asleep face down at the beach after one too many mojitos.

My friends—future enemies—placed two peach halves and a banana on my back. Classic.

When I woke up hours later, I had a perfectly tanned body… except for one very obvious shape burned in negative.

The result?

A giant sunburned back with the pale outline of a full-blown fruit-based penis.

For the rest of the trip, every time I took my shirt off, people either gasped, laughed, or asked if it was a modern art piece.

One guy asked if it was a tribute. I

 said, "Yes. To betrayal."

I spent the rest of the trip trying to even it out.

Spoiler: I couldn't.

I looked like I had a shadow sponsor from OnlyFans.

MYKONOS MADE ME DO IT

FAQ #10: What is the future of Mykonos?

First of all, Mykonos is a survivor. The island has lived through pirate raids, economic crises, over-tourism scandals, and even the Kardashians — and every time, it reinvented itself.

What's next?

- **More regulation:** The days of undeclared villas and "anything goes" business are fading. Tax audits, building restrictions, and stricter licensing are tightening the game.

- **Higher prices:** The island is already expensive, but expect it to climb even further. Fewer people, bigger wallets — that's the strategy.

- **Shift in crowd:** The diversity that once made Mykonos exciting is fading. Instead of a mix, it's increasingly the same type of rich people — older, image-obsessed, and more concerned with posts and views than with fun.

- **Sustainability pressure:** The island is bursting at the seams. Traffic jams, water shortages, and power cuts already strain the infrastructure. Unless Mykonos invests heavily in sustainability, it risks collapsing under its own success.

The risk:

But let's be honest: the Mykonos that became legendary wasn't born from luxury boutiques or Instagram-friendly sunsets. It was born from chaos. The streets used to be insane — Italians at toga parties, drag queens strutting through Chora, people having sex outdoors in dark corners, fashions that made no sense, and attitudes that made even less. Every night was an unpredictable happening. You never knew what you'd see — and the next day, you couldn't believe the stories from last night.

That madness is what made Mykonos famous. Today, though, the vibe has shifted. It's all quite preppy: the fashion, the behavior, the nightlife. Everything is *comme il faut*, polished and perfect for the front page of *The New York Times*. But the real fun, the unforgettable memories? Those don't fit on Instagram — and Mykonos used to be too much for Instagram to ever capture.

And here lies the danger: Mykonos could follow the path of other once-sexy destinations — Cannes, Saint-Tropez, even parts of Miami. These places thrived on youth, beauty, and spontaneity. But when prices soared, the young disappeared. Without them, the lust and energy disappeared too.

Older visitors want to be surrounded by youth — it's what keeps a place vibrant. When that disappears, escorts fill the gap. But escorts are predictable. First, they're the same faces you could meet back home. Second, it's a business transaction — not lust, not chaos, not fun, not magic. Without youth-driven spontaneity, even the rich eventually get bored and move on to the next place that still feels wild and alive.

The truth? Mykonos has survived before, and it can survive again — but only if it keeps its pulse. If it becomes all price and no passion, it risks irrelevance. If it finds a way to balance glamour with madness *and* sustainability, then it will remain what it has been for 80 years: one of the world's most desired islands.

"HEY! OH… WAIT."

I saw her across the tables and froze. That face. I knew her. Definitely.

My brain kicked into overdrive. Villa party? A friend's ex? That girl who borrowed my charger at Scorpios?

She looked right at me.

I panicked and did what felt safest—waved. Big smile. Confident nod. The "we've definitely shared gossip over overpriced rosé" wave.

She paused… then waved back. Full wave. Big smile. Like we were old friends.

And that's when the real torture began.

I had no idea who she was. Now I had seconds to figure it out before someone asked.

My table went silent. I could feel ten pairs of sunglasses turning toward me. One friend leaned in:

"Wait… how do you know her?"

My brain flipped through every beach club, afterparty, WhatsApp group, and random drunk DM.

Nothing. Absolutely nothing.

Then my friend's boyfriend choked on his drink.

"Dude," he said, eyes wide. "That's Cleo Vixen."

The name meant nothing—until someone showed me her Instagram.

And then… other sites.

She was an adult film star. Famous. Like, very famous.

And she had just waved back at me like we were brunch besties.

The entire section went quiet. People stared at me.

One guy actually moved his sunglasses down to look at me with his bare eyes.

And I had to sit there, pretending I wasn't the guy who just confidently claimed friendship with someone he'd only ever seen in… professionally compromised scenarios.

I didn't order dessert.

I ordered the bill. And maybe a new face.

MYKONOS MADE ME DO IT

CONCLUSION

Mykonos Made Me Do It: It truly did

If you've made it this far, you've probably realized something: Mykonos isn't just a destination. It's a character — flawed, outrageous, magnetic, sometimes exhausting, but impossible to ignore.

It's the island that has made people fall in love, lose their minds, waste fortunes, create memories, and swear they'll never come back… only to return the next summer. It's a survivor, constantly reinventing itself, balancing between chaos and order, between lust and luxury, between being too much and never enough.

Mykonos is not for everyone. And that's the point. The island doesn't exist to please you — you adapt to it. You play its game. Sometimes you win, sometimes you lose, but you always leave with a story.

After 35 summers here, I can tell you this: the real Mykonos doesn't live in Instagram posts or hotel brochures. It lives in the energy you feel walking through Chora at 4 a.m., in the sand sticking to your skin after a night swim, in the laugh of a stranger you'll never see again.

Mykonos will outlive the trends, the scandals, the influencers, and even this book. Because Mykonos doesn't care about being loved. It only cares about being unforgettable.

ABOUT THE AUTHOR

Dimitris Margetas was born in Greece and has lived in six countries around the world. He studied Chemistry and Civil Engineering, and spent twenty years working in marketing. Today he is the owner of a chain of souvlaki restaurants in Switzerland, where he has lived permanently since 2002, while spending his summers between Athens and Mykonos.

He has served as a judge at the Miss Universe pageant, written successful songs, and manages viral social media accounts. At the same time, he writes books inspired by the contrasts of modern life in Greece — and beyond.

And yes — Mykonos made him do this book too.

Printed in Dunstable, United Kingdom

69007339R00067